~ From Cages to Couches ~

The true histories within this book introduce thirty animals, saved & rehabilitated by **BEAGLE FREEDOM PROJECT**, all fully in love with their caregivers

A collection of heartfelt stories directly from the families of these "Freagles" & "Frounds"

compiled by Kris Wood

BEAGLE FREEDOM PROJECT *was formed to rescue these animals and bring an end to testing all together*

Forward-

Every day, at any given moment, there are approximately 65,000 dogs suffering in United States laboratories. Most people do not know this. Why? Because the animal testing industry hides behind the billions of dollars they make through testing, and spend it on advertising to make the consumer believe that animal testing is necessary and that really "only" rats, mice and rabbits are used for testing.

Nothing could be further from the truth. Dogs, just like the ones we share our homes with, are bred in a commercial breeding facility to be sold into research, or, they are victims of pound seizure, taken from a pound before their kill date and sold to testing.

These dogs never see the light of day. Many have never been outside. Ever. Never touched the grass. Never played with a toy or know the taste of a treat. They don't get snuggles on the couch or fun things to see and do.

Instead, they are kept in cold, steel cages, alone, and usually in a basement, where they are given nothing, and only see the torture ahead of them.

They are branded with a federal ID number tattooed in their ear and that is all they are known by. Many times, their vocal cords are cut so they do not "disturb" the laboratory workers.

They are tested on cleaning products, illegal drugs, pharmaceuticals and more. However, in the United States it is not mandatory to test cosmetics and many products on animals, but huge corporations still do so. It is cruel. It is unnecessary. It is unethical; and it is just plain wrong.

Beagle Freedom Project was formed to rescue those animals and advocate for an end to testing all together.

When I first found out about animal testing, I was appalled. I have devoted my entire life to ending testing, but had no idea I would actually be able to rescue animals suffering in laboratories.

In December of 2010, I was fortunate to receive information about dogs who needed rescue in a lab and I jumped at the chance!

In my mind, I pictured freeing the dogs for the first time, and seeing them run with joy and excitement. But, when I saw them, a sad reality made my heart sink. These beagles had never been outside of a lab, they never had exercise, they had never seen the sunshine. When I met them, they were shaking and salivating in their cages, standing in their own urine and feces. They had shave marks on their bodies.

I brought them to a secure yard to release them, but when I opened their cages, they would not step foot outside. They were so frightened of the outside world, they just stood there.

It took over 20 minutes to coax the first beagle out of his cage. When he finally did take his first step of freedom, he was wobbly and could barely walk, from lack of muscle tone. It wasn't until I walked over to the other beagle, still shaking in his cage, and touched his nose, that the other one gingerly took his first steps outside.

The realization that these dogs are so neglected and abused and HIDDEN was awakening. I had no idea how hard it would be for them to adjust to the outside world. But they did…. And since then, hundreds of others we have rescued have done just that. They have not only adjusted, but thrived and are LOVING LIFE.

Instead of the federal ID number tattooed in their ears, they have a name, a family and a life. In this book, you will be fortunate enough to read about the rescue of many beagles from animal testing, and transformations they made from being "test subject" to family member.

Kris Woods' account in her first book, "From Cage to Couch" told the story of Chief, rescued from a laboratory in Spain and the bond that was formed and the lessons learned.

"From Cages to Couches" will explore the rescue of many other beagles from testing and advocate for them through their stories of facing fears, exploring the real world, forming family bonds, and finding the comfort in finally being able to live life as every dog should.

- Shannon Keith, Esq. President & Founder, Beagle Freedom Project

Acknowledgements - Gweneth DeHaven – cover and collage artwork

Memorial –

Is it ever long enough with a beloved pet? I, and many like me, would have to say no. I don't know if it makes these losses harder because of the circumstances from which these souls come to us or simply because they have become such loved and important parts of our lives.

These are just some of the many faces BEAGLE FREEDOM PROJECT has lost since it began rescuing animals from laboratories. These are the many faces of the tortured souls that were held behind the closed doors of those laboratories. These are also the many faces of the animals that were rehabilitated into loving family members through love, caring, and the patience of their amazing people.

No longer numbers, but names with personalities, quirks, favorites, and fears of their own. We will miss them dearly but they will always have a place in our hearts and fuel the need to keep working until all cages are empty. - Kris Wood, author, From Cage to Couch

From Cages to Couches

Table of Contents

Cate

I used to be identified as the branded tattooed number in my ear. Let me properly introduce myself. I am Cate. Also known as "Cate the Great". My family will never know where I came from or the history of pain that I have endured. They only know my behavior, what I believe your society refers to as PTSD. After being labeled "experimentally spent" I was released underweight with sunken, lifeless eyes.

When I first came to my new family, I would rest my head against a wall and refuse to look at anyone or come out of hiding places. I was petrified, burying my head further than I thought possible. They knew this was not typical beagle behavior. You see, they had my new beagle brother, Buddy for 12 years. It was Buddy that saved me, taught me how to be a dog, taught me how to be their family.

My new Mom would tell me repeatedly that I would not be hurt anymore, but I was very skeptical. I would shake when I was around stairs. I was at war with myself transitioning between rooms. When I ate, I would stretch out very long, grab food recoiling quickly, always looking over my shoulder. I would growl at Buddy over water. I saw mom's broken face and heard "what was done to you?" Little by little, I started to see that this family wasn't going to hurt me. I opened up. I still had a reluctant eye and sometimes reverted back to my old hiding places, but I wouldn't stay there as long.

And then I started doing what a lot of humans are incapable of-I started to overcome my past. I learned to trust, forgive, and most importantly, love. Every day I grow stronger. I zoom up and down the stairs. I knock my Nana over with kisses when she comes for a visit. I pounce on my mom's lap whether she is prepared for me or not. I playfully chase the kids and steal their balls. I hang my head out the window in the car and be free. I am free.

Every morning my mom says to me, "It's another day. Another day out of that lab." And I roll around wagging my tail begging for a tummy rub. You can find me snuggled up to my human brothers and sister or stretched out on mom and dad's bed. I am no longer a means to an end. I am no longer a number. I am free, I am family, I am loved . . . I am Cate.

Chief

I first heard about the "Spanish 40" rescue from my mom; she had seen a quick story on the news about them. I mentioned to my husband we should try to adopt one…not really thinking what it would involve. The story intrigued me, rescuing 40 laboratory test beagles from a medical testing facility in Spain that were going to be killed if no one stepped up to take them in. **Enter Beagle Freedom Project.**

After many attempts to get in contact with BFP we finally set up the meeting to see #7, George Clooney, Bagel. He was skinny to say the least. He skulked around the yard with his tail between his legs, always looking over his shoulder. He would come over occasionally and put his front paws on our legs for a pat, but then quickly leave once we gave him one. He bolted if a noise was too loud and if one of us stood up too quickly near him. We loaded him into the truck and headed home for the beginning of his new life!

#7 became **Chief**, The Beef, Chiefer Beefers, the Cheetah and a multitude of other nick names. We discovered he had no idea how to eat or drink from a bowl, wag his tail, play, cuddle, act with other dogs, and just plain be a dog. He was scared of doorways, loud noises, sudden movements, anything over his head like ceiling fans, rain, and being held. It broke my heart to watch him scoot and run away from us even when we were trying to give him affection.

After months of constant attention, affection, and exposure to everything we could find Chief has become a well-adjusted, loving, smush of a beagle. He loves to hunt squirrels, chase cars, curl up on the couch, and eat! He travels to Montana every summer where he swims, explores, rolls in smelly dead stuff, and eats!

Laboratories try to say these dogs cannot be rehabilitated so they must be killed…I say, they couldn't be more wrong. Just look at Chief!

I hope you love it! ♡ Kris & Chief

4

Klein

Looking at Klein today, no one would ever know what a scared mess he was the day he came to live with us.

The day Klein arrived, he was extremely fearful. The first few days were rough. He wouldn't let me or my husband touch him, growling and barking at us, but he followed me everywhere, including to the bathroom. I tried every once in a while to pet him to no avail. After the first week, he began letting me get a quick touch in every few times that I tried. He began allowing me to touch him more than a single time as the days went on. About a month into it, I sat down on the floor to pet him, and he rolled over and showed me his belly. I cried as I gave him a belly rub.

Today, there are very few traces of the scared Klein that came to live with us. Klein happily and confidently spends his days wrestling with his sister, Tora; has completely commandeered one our couches for daily naps so much that we routinely refer to it as "Klein's couch"; sleeps in bed with us every night, and is a world traveler, usually traveling to our other home in Belize.

Watching Klein in our travels and while in Belize always brings a smile to our faces. He struts through airports as if he owns them, sleeps confidently at our feet until we land, and is always insanely excited to see the water taxi that will take us to our other home. He spends his days in Belize trying to figure out what the crabs are doing all over our sandy yard; prowling the beach looking for items to sniff, sunning himself on our deck; and full on launching into the water from the dock. He confidently swims in the ocean, using his tail as a very effective rudder.

Klein gets the most joy from his rides into the village on the golf cart sporting his bright red sunglasses, hanging his head over the side and taking in all the sights and smells. He has ensured that the locals have fallen in love with him. Klein seems the happiest in Belize, transforming into "Zen dog". We absolutely love when it is time to travel to Belize and we get to ask him, "Bubba, are you ready to go to the beach house?" His reaction is one of sheer joy, barking, jumping, and whining. We have always joked that the title of a book written about Klein would be, "From Cage to Caribbean Canine".

Nelly

December 3rd, 2014 a couple driving down a quiet road in the Florida panhandle spotted a crate just off the side of the road. They stopped to inspect and what they found horrified them. Inside the crate were 3 beagles, all had been shot and were covered in blood. Two were already dead, but one still barely clung to life. All 3 dogs had the telltale markings tattooed inside their ears signifying they had been in a laboratory. The survivor was rushed to the vet where Beagle Freedom Project was contacted. The brave little beagle was named Nelly.

A thorough examination of Nelly showed a history of neglect, abuse and sickness. Her teeth were worn to nubs from chewing on the metal cages and she had a large mammary tumor that needed to be removed. After surgery, it was confirmed that the tumor was cancer.

On January 15th, I drove from Jacksonville to Port St. Joe to meet Nelly. When I first arrived I was met by a little ball of energy with a cone on her head and surgery drain tubes in her abdomen. I was astounded by how much spunk this little girl had for what she had just gone through. I was immediately in love and knew my life was about to be changed forever.

A few weeks after she came home, she developed an infection due to complications with the tumor removal surgery. Still, she persevered and fought the sickness and got healthy. Then in May, we were dealt another devastating blow. She went into complete liver failure. I sat in the vet's office bawling. Her liver values were so high the vet gave her a 20% chance of survival. But she was a fighter; she wasn't ready to give up. She spent an entire week at the vet, and every day she got stronger. She waited for me to come see her every afternoon, which I did. And she survived.

Nelly learned to trust people and forgive the abuse that she suffered for over a decade in captivity. She was truly an inspiration. However, Nelly crossed the Rainbow Bridge on September 10, 2017 due to complications from her time in the lab. My heart is broken.

Franklin

In August 2013, I met a beagle that changed my life. Number 4 boldly approached me, resting his head on my knee. His tail wagged and I became a foster fail. Number 4 became Franklin of the Bay Area 6. At 17 pounds, he was a little guy with a big personality. As experienced beagle owners, we thought we were prepared. We weren't.

Franklin arrived grossly underweight with a dull, shedding coat. He wasn't interested in food or water and froze when touched. When held, he extended his neck as if submitting to a tube or blood draw. Franklin made no sounds and hid when frightened. The early months were challenging. Franklin was difficult to housetrain due to his life in a cage. He had a dangerous obsession of swallowing socks and was a terrible hoarder. He hated walks and had frequent night terrors.

Franklin was an escape artist. Within weeks, I spent $400 "McGyvering" pens, gates, and screens. He never hopped over, but pulled, pushed, or busted through whatever confined him. He was a genius, determined to be free. He was also socially awkward. Franklin stared, which was interpreted as aggression. My older border collie, annoyed by his nonsense, took it upon herself to teach Franklin manners.

Despite early challenges, Franklin is an amazing beagle. He enjoys walks, and is fearless and friendly. He doesn't howl, stray, or chase squirrels. No longer afraid to be touched, Franklin throws himself against you for snuggles. Although debarked, he manages a hoarse, yet cheerful bark. Franklin has given up socks and loves his food.

Franklin is an avid spokesbeagle for BFP. He attended fundraisers, posed for photos, staffed booths, and travelled to Sacramento to lobby for the Beagle Freedom Bill. Franklin has met Federal and State Legislators and dignitaries. I tell them bluntly that Franklin was supposed to die and was considered a petri dish to be discarded. That always starts a conversation. And because of Franklin, we have changed how we live and the products we consume. Thanks, BFP for transforming all our lives for the better.

Ike

It all started three years ago. I was walking my beagle, Molly, when we can across an older couple walking their two beagles. We immediately stopped to talk. I think all beagle owners have that innate connection; like long-lost family members. The first thing I noticed immediately was that their dogs were not "typical" beagles. One was somewhat friendly, but the other hid behind his owner's leg. The owners saw the query in my face and proceeded to tell me about the Beagle Freedom Project. This conversation about their beagles opened my eyes, my heart, and changed my life.

I walked back to my house and immediately filled out the application on the BFP website. As a side note, I had just lost my beagle, Sabra, to cancer. I swore to myself that Molly was my only and last Beagle. Those feelings changed after seeing those beagles and hearing their story. About a month later, we received a call about adoption. I was nervous, but also very excited. My husband and I decided to go through with the screening process. I remember it felt like an eternity waiting those few days after the home visit until they made the decision to allow us to adopt Ike.

I remember the day I picked Ike up and took him home-June 18, 2014. He sat so nicely on the passenger seat next to me on the journey to his new home. It was as if he knew how happy and safe he would be. On the first night, he would not eat. That changed very quickly. We also learned very early on, that if a door or gate was open he would be off and running. We definitely had a few narrow escapes.

Ike, the Hollywood hound, is a puppy at heart. He is always rolling on the floor for belly rubs and kisses. I do not think he ever stops wagging his tail. He also loves to show his pearly whites, smiling all the time. My husband plays a game with him by howling and Ike happily mimics the howls. My daughters dress him up in their old baby clothes with him loving every minute of it. Lastly, Ike and Molly (non-BFP) are like two peas in a pod. Thank you Beagle Freedom Project for rescuing my Ike and letting us love him in his forever home.

Dean

Words can hardly describe how traumatized Dean was from his experience as a laboratory animal. He was 18 months old when he was rescued and he came to our family a scarred dog. He hated people. He was not aggressive, but his evil eye look said, "Stay away." He also had puppy tendencies and needed to chew. We gave him toys and chews, but nothing tasted better than the furniture, walls, and rugs. He was impossible to catch, so we kept a leash on him in the house and retrieved him when necessary.

Dean was adopted three years ago and it took him two years to develop trust. For Dean, everything was baby steps. Luke helped Dean adjust as they cuddled together on the couch and bed. Our black lab taught Dean to play tug-of-war with toys and Calamity was a role model of how a well behaved dog acts.

As much as we loved Dean and wished that he loved us, he needed time and space. Eventually, he let us pet him in a safe place on the couch. He liked to ride in the car, so we took him many places. We drove him to Sacramento as an Ambassadog for the California Beagle Freedom Bill. There he walked in a rally and was photographed with movie star and producer Nikki Reed. Next, Dean traveled to Las Vegas for a reunion of his rescue group "The Lucky 9." Then, he traveled to Carson City with Luke to meet and greet in front of the State Capitol and attend the hearings for the Nevada Beagle Freedom Bill. He has an amazing nose and attended "sniffing" classes where he had to find hidden food. He was the star of his class.

It took a long time, but Dean's developed trust. He is now our sweet boy who adores his home and family. He gets so excited when we come home and gives a special dance. He begs for his treats of carrots and green beans and we cannot refuse. Loving Dean did not change the world, but it changed his world forever.

Cheryl Doetch

Dean's Mom

Photo Sarah Jane Hardt

Peyton

While on vacation last summer I received a call from BFP asking if we could foster a dog that was a bit tougher than some of the other dogs released with him. Besides the awful testing he endured, he had also suffered an injury to his leg when the laboratory staff got it caught in the cage door.

I figured we would work with Peyton for a couple of months and then help him become adopted. I also found out that we were not his first foster family. My son and I went to the release party to pick him up in July of last year. Peyton was extremely wary of people that day but he actually was a great passenger in the car. He did not display any symptoms of car anxiety that our first rescue beagle did.

When we got home he immediately ran to the back of the house and hid in our bathroom. That was his safe place for some weeks until he became a bit more trusting. Just like Woody, our first rescue, Peyton became very attached to Ruby, our Labrador. We call her the dog whisperer because both beagles love her very much and do not want her to be out of their sight.

At first Peyton had many issues. He frequently urinated in the house, could not have the door shut to the backyard, was very frightened of any male figures in the house, couldn't walk on a leash (he would chew through it) and loud noises frightened him terribly.

When it came time to discuss whether or not he was ready for adoption we knew that he needed us as much as we need him, so we became proud foster failures. Peyton continues to have some struggles, he has had three seizures and is currently on anti-seizure medication, but he also has had some amazing breakthroughs!

After almost being with us for a year, he has decided that he wants to go on walks with Woody and Ruby! He no longer urinates in the house, he lets us give him a bath, he is very playful and loves to have snacks (especially cheese). We are so happy to have him in our family!

Elwood (Woody)

One afternoon in late October 2015, my husband and I were driving to lunch when we spotted a Beagle Freedom Project sticker on the bumper of a car. We had no idea what this organization was so we decided to research it while we were eating. Two months later we drove to Las Vegas to Cheryl and Donnie Hall's house, BFP adopters and foster parents, to have our Labrador, Ruby, meet Elwood.

We had been wanting to get a friend for Ruby, and once we had researched the website we were hooked. Elwood was part of the Summer of 38 rescue group. When he first was released he was one of the most anxiety ridden dogs of the group. Woody, as Donnie nicknamed him, would spin excessively counter-clockwise only, was frightened to come through doors or eat his food. He had to have a rope attached to his collar just so that he could be caught to come in at night. My husband and I loved him immediately! We all got him packed into his thunder shirt, took a whole roll of paper towels (Cheryl let us know he drools in the car) and we were off for home.

It has now been a year and a half and Woody and the BFP has changed our lives. He is still scared at loud sounds, unfamiliar people, trash cans and other random things. He hates riding in the car and still drools and occasionally throws up. However, even though he still does spin, it usually out of excitement. He loves to go on walks, chase balls, eat carrots and play with Ruby and our newest addition, Peyton.

Woody is one of the loves of my life and is continuing to heal from his ordeal in the laboratory. He did have a setback when he hurt his back and was diagnosed with a calcified disc but he has bounced back. He is happiest when we are all home (especially Ruby) and he can sleep on the couch in peace. He has made great strides since being released and we are so grateful to have the opportunity to be his adopted family!

Cash

Cash came home with us on October 5, 2013. He was one of the "Memphis 7". He would not eat, would not drink, and was not potty trained. Thankfully, he got along with all of my other dogs. He also took to sleeping in the bed, curled up right next to my belly. He had no idea what a leash was and just rolled over on his back when we tried to walk him. We fed him and gave him water out of a cup for the first week. Every noise made him hide or pace the floor.

He was so nervous. It made me so incredibly sad to see the fear in this precious dog's eyes and imagine what had happened to him.

Over time, he began to relax, fatten up and became one of the pack. He has some stomach issues where he will get very nauseated and continuously lick the floor and about a year after we got him, he started having seizures. When we had him examined by the vet, they also found a large incision on his belly that had staples at one point. He also has horrible teeth. Cash is only 6 and has had his teeth cleaned twice and lost 21 teeth so far. His teeth are unusually fragile and soft, likely also medication related.

Cash lives with his six other dog siblings. One of which is, Clarabelle, a 3-legged ARME rescue. His favorite things are food, laying on the couch or bed, and laying under his tree outside. He is the sweetest, most affectionate dog I have. He is overly attached to me and howls anytime I leave the house. It's ok... I am overly attached to him to. Some think we rescued him but, I truly believe he rescued me. He taught me more compassion, an appreciation for the little things in life, and opened my heart even wider.

Our lives are forever changed because of him. We love him so much. I am so glad BFP entrusted him with us. I will forever fight for these animals.

Liberty

We saw the first signs of life returning to our Liberty, when she met her dog sister, Minnie. Liberty immediately got pep in her step and the dogs spent the next few hours frolicking throughout our house. In short, she lived.

Things we take for granted as understood behaviors or abilities for a dog were not for Liberty. At first, she would not eat. She could not drink from a bowl. Treats? She turned her nose at them, never knowing how yummy they could be. Simply walking was difficult. She couldn't walk on the leash, even around the house and definitely not outside. Thankfully, Minnie was a great teacher and with each moment, trust was gained, and no skill was left unattained.

Despite the great strides Liberty has made in the past11 months, she is replaced by the dog formally known as 0220423 every time an unfamiliar person or object comes near her. Liberty will instantaneously shut down if presented with something or someone unknown. She will shake, bow her head to avoid eye contact, and at times, return to playing dead, refusing to go near the unfamiliar thing. Liberty still has nightmares of the horrible experiences she endured. She shakes and salivates when it is time for her to receive food. Her teeth are ground down to nubs from trying to escape her captivity. She cannot go to dog parks because the bars necessary to protect and keep her safe, remind her of a time she was anything but. The sound of a passing motorcycle during a walk causes her to cower on the ground, eyes closed and shaking.

With more time and love, Liberty will continue to flourish. To a passerby as we walk down the street, you would not know she was once contained in a world of pain and loneliness. However, if you were to look inside her oversized floppy ears you would find her tattoo, a forever reminder in the ear of this creature I love. I hope one day this mark and her memories from that terrible time in her life will fade, visible only to those who know where to look.

Baxter

Baxter's journey began as one of the Prairie State Pups rescued in New Jersey in September 2016. He was one of seven including Candy, Alaska, Chunky, Leo, Harley, and Teddy. In the beginning it was tough as he was very hesitant to leave his cage.

After leaving the lab, Baxter joined his fosters Donna and John in Illinois. They were very loving and helped Baxter adjust to life outside. They began potty training and helping him learn how to "dog".

In December, Sevon and Jolen received the call! Baxter was ready to go to his forever home and they were picked to become mom and dad! Baxter made the trip up to Northern Minnesota and he initially was not a fan of the -20 temperatures at his new home! Baxter has two playmates, Bogey and Birdi, and a big, fenced yard to run in. While it took Baxter a bit to warm up to dad, he instantly loved his mom and clung to her a lot. He had a little trouble with stairs and would "freeze up" on hard surfaces though that becomes less with each day.

Baxter has come out of his shell and is now like a puppy! He has learned to sit, shake, sit-up, and speak both little and big speaks! He loves to go outside and run around his yard, barking at the neighbors if he catches a glance through the fence. Baxter loves to play with Birdi and has even helped whip her into shape. He is starting to be interested in toys and will chase after them, but doesn't bring them back yet. He has also discovered the treat drawer and a love for venison!

Every morning, Baxter loves to wake up his mom by pawing at her face playfully so she knows it's time to get up! When dad gets home, Baxter jumps up to be held and hugged, which he loves. At night, he climbs up his puppy stairs into bed and sleeps between mom and dad. He is now living the good life and the lab is just a distant memory!

Freya

I had been waiting for months for "the call" to be a foster for Beagle Freedom Project. I received the call and was asked "Do you mind if she is not a beagle?" I said of course I don't mind she will be perfect I'm sure! I was also told she was an older girl who had spent 12 years in the lab. 12 years, my heart broke for this girl, what had she endured?

Driving to meet her I could not contain my excitement. When the van door opened there she was, so scared and unsure. The thing that struck me right away was how regal she was. Although she was visibly terrified she held her head high and looked me in the eyes. Those big beautiful brown eyes melted my heart and stole my soul that very second. As I put her in my car to take her home I whispered in her ear "I've got you sweet girl. You don't have to be afraid, you're safe now." I knew then she was home.

We started like most BFP rescues. She didn't know what grass was, didn't know how to drink from a bowl, the usual gauntlet of terror. By day two we noticed some abnormalities. Freya was having medical issues. We rushed her to the vet. The worst possible news was delivered. Freya had major medical issues. The vet said two weeks to two months was the best we could hope for. Devastated we took her home determined to make the best of what little time we would have. We had 13 different prescriptions, several holistic aides and a very special home cooked diet.

Freya was a fighter and it was obvious she wanted to live. She became a loved member of our family. She learned to be a dog, to play, to love attention and affection. She would come to me and lay her head in my lap for gentle caresses. She was happy and we denied her nothing. She loved beds so I filled the house, porches, and yard with them. Her favorite spot was on the porch where she could lie in the sun. Months went by and my regal queen was happy. Sadly, she had a very aggressive cancer that took her from us on December 28, 2016. We had our girl for 15 months but she will be in our hearts forever. Love always wins!

Bee

I was on the BFP website to sponsor an Identity Campaign dog. After a few minutes of not finding what I was looking for, I decide to go ahead a fill out the foster/adopt form. I figured it would take years to hear back. Two weeks is all it took. When I got the call I panicked, I wasn't ready for another dog, we had 5, our oldest was 12 and getting pretty cranky, and I didn't want to upend his twilight years.

Monique told me there were a lot of dogs coming out of the lab at once and some were pretty close to us. She convinced me maybe we should foster. I asked Jimmy if he wanted to foster a beagle. I knew he would say yes, he always says yes to new dogs. When he found out it was a BFP dog, he absolutely wanted to keep her. No, we are going to take this dog, teach it how to be a dog and then give it to a family that will love it forever.

Bee comes to our house and it is pure chaos. She wants nothing to do with the people in the house but she does like the other dogs. The old guy isn't to upset about her being there and she folds nicely into the pack. My resolve is still strong, we are going to teach her how to be a dog and then give her to her family. Luckily her "safe spot" was on the love seat. She could see all entryways from that spot and kept a close eye and where everyone was at all times. For two weeks we could hardly touch her. Slowly she realized we weren't going to hurt her and she would tolerate some gentle pats. I spent hours on that love seat with her just quietly sitting there, stealing some pets when I could.

One day she slid closer to me, wanting to be petted. Before I knew it, she slid into my lap. I was so excited I didn't know what to do. She willingly crawled into my lap and wanted my attention. While I was stroking her velvet ears I was quietly talking to her. I told her she was safe, no one would ever hurt her again, that I would defend her with my life if I had to, she would only know love and kindness for the rest of her life.

I promised her all of these things and more. Bee put her head on my shoulder and let out a giant sigh, it was the sweetest sound that I had ever heard. Before long I realized I was crying, I was crying because I was so happy she trusted me, I was crying because I was so sad for what she had endured, I was crying because I was angry that there were so many other dogs in cages not sitting on love seats. When I told Jimmy we were keeping her he laughed and told me "we were always going to keep her."

We taught her how to be a dog and we did find a family who would love her forever, our family, and it was one of the best decisions we ever made. Sweet little buzzy, buzzy, bumble Bee, our home wouldn't be the same without her.

Bocce

I found Beagle Freedom Project on Facebook and wanted to follow the good work they do. I donated after being educated and believing in their Mission. I somehow convinced my husband that I would fill out the foster form thinking we would never get the call. I agreed to listen to the details of the most recent rescue in Northern CA and was curious about those Beagles that were now on their way to Southern CA. And then…I said "Yes".

I will likely never forget the day Number 7 came into my life, December 13, 2016. It was a day filled with high emotion, cautious energy and utter disbelief. My mom and I drove the 40 plus miles from my home in Orange County CA to Los Angeles to meet the Beagles now called the SoCal Snowflakes. I had agreed to foster one and promised my husband that I would only get a female being that I already had two female Beagles at home.

The drive was long in LA traffic and gave me too much time to think about what these little pups had endured. I didn't know anything as no information related to the rescue had or would be released. We were asked not to post anything on social media until given the ok to do so. Everything felt so secret and therefore so much scarier.

We arrived at the home that was facilitating the process ready to meet this group of newly rescued Beagles. I walked up the driveway as instructed and entered the yard. I immediately saw a male Beagle, tail tucked and head down, #7 hand written on his new collar. He had a reddish tint all over his body especially on his paws, his ears were so dirty and he smelled. As I scanned him, I noticed the freckles on his nose. That was the end for me! I sat on the ground, put my hand out, and he tentatively approached. He never looked into my eyes but I knew, he was the one. I didn't meet any of the other dogs that day and it was ok. Bocce was waiting at that gate for me…and the rest is history!

I drove back down that freeway with my new baby in my lap and knew that we had a long road ahead of us but I was sure we were going to be just fine, especially when the foster process "failed" a month later. At 4 years old, he had to learn how to drink water from a bowl, take a treat from my hand, use the stairs, lay on something soft and walk on a leash. But, we wouldn't have it any other way. Bocce has a permanent place in my heart, my home, and in the pack.

Baxter Boo

Baxter was the bad boy of Beagle Freedom Project Rescue #11, the Midwest 10. He had difficulty getting along with other dogs and went through 3 foster homes. The day he arrived at my house he peed at the front door, wandered through every room, peed at the back door and then took a nap in the sun. He was HOME.

Baxter is not the bad boy any longer. My neighbors call him the best behaved dog on the neighborhood. He's smart, sensitive, stubborn, and curious. In other words, all things beagle.

Baxter loves all creatures, especially kitties. He and Rufus were best friends. After Rufus passed, Baxter and I adopted another beagle out of a high kill shelter. We named her Tashi which means "luck" in Tibetan. Now, he's the one teaching her the ropes.

Baxter loves going on adventures more than anything, except food. He loves hiking in Griffith Park and trips to the beach. Living in LA has its perks and we've run into a few celebrities while out on "urban adventures". Baxter wasn't impressed when we met Denzel Washington, but I was. Baxter thinks he's the star of the neighborhood.

Being a beagle, he loves food. His favorites are chicken, sweet potatoes and steamed veggies. He LOVES pizza crust, but hates fruit.

He has a few special toys, but his favorite thing is a good game of chase.

Baxter still has a few little quirks. He's afraid of blankets and towels and is terrified of the sound of keys jangling. He also won't let anyone he doesn't know pet him. He's getting better with that though. If he senses it's OK with me and you get down low and offer a treat, he'll allow you to adore him. There's a price to pay for his love.

I've had many dogs throughout the years, but he's my heart and soul. I vowed when I adopted him that I would make every day out of the lab his very best day ever. And I do.

Dillan

In late 2014, my husband and I filled out an application to adopt a beagle through Beagle Freedom Project. 0n February 11, 2015 I was contacted via email by the adoption coordinator for Beagle Freedom Project asking if I was interested in meeting a 3 year old Coonhound who had recently been rescued from a laboratory. I was stoked! After a few email exchanges a meet and greet with us and our two beagles was set up with Eric, who would come to be known as Dillan aka Dill Pickles.

The first time I met Dillan, I instantly fell in love with him. He had these big brown Soulful eyes and long floppy ears. I knew in my heart of hearts he belonged with us. During our drive home, my husband and I decided Dillan would become a part of our family. On February 15, 2015 we returned to his foster mom's house and picked up our boy.

Once Dillan was home with us he wouldn't eat his food unless I added treats. He had a brand new bed, but would sleep curled up on the floor behind the front door. It broke my heart. But after a few days he began to use his bed eat his food without treats and he began to play. I even found him sleeping on our bed!

Dillan has come a long way in the 2 years he's been free. Loud noises, like the garbage truck that once scared him out of his sleep now don't seem to startle him. He enjoys running around the yard chasing his siblings, and has become a professional beggar with the hopes he'll get a taste of your food. He's become my sidekick in the kitchen while I cook.

He's has had two birthday parties and experienced unwrapping presents on Christmas morning. Yes! He's spoiled! But what can I say? Dillan endured a life of only hurt and pain, prior to his home with us, so I will give him a life of unconditional love and spoiling. Because after all …
THIS IS WHAT FREEDOM LOOKS LIKE!

Paulie

ECF1. That was his identifier, a tattoo in his ear. I won't even call it a name because that would mean that those monsters actually cared about him.

On December 13, 2013 Beagle Freedom Project came to the rescue and saved our little man along with 8 other Beagles from a laboratory. Once they made the trek from the lab to the release party they were all given collars and names. He was now, after 3 ½ years in a cage, finally going to have a name. Paulie.

We weren't Paulie's first home. We got a call on December 23 to see if we could take him as a foster. Of course, we jumped at the chance. My husband and our Basset, Tommy went to pick him up on Christmas Eve. He would prove to be the best Christmas present we ever received.

Paulie's first act when he got to our house was to take a big, runny poop on the living room carpet. My heart sank because I knew he was scared.

Over the next days we made him part of our routine. He ate when our other dog ate, went for walks with us, and had his very first Christmas. We were only supposed to watch him for a few days, but when his adoption fell through with another family, we pounced.

In the months that followed he learned to poop outside, sing for his supper, beg for snacks, and play. He also showed himself to be a world class snuggler.

Fast forward 3 ½ years from his release and Paulie is a happy, typical Beagle. He loves to shred paper, chew up plastic bottles, steal things that aren't his, and tease his Basset brother by making the short guy chase him around the yard.

Our lives are forever changed after seeing the progression from scared laboratory animal to a confident, silly, sweet family dog.

Charlotte

My name is Charlotte. It was dark. And loud. There were so many other dogs. I was in a cage with another dog I had never seen or smelled before. I was scared.

And then it was light. And the cage door opened up to this soft, green stuff as far as I could see. There were people and they were all watching us to see what we would do. I took a step. And then another step. And then more steps. And then I ran. I was FREE!

Up until that moment, I had spent every minute of my short 10 months of life living in a cage inside a dark laboratory. I had never seen grass or the sun or been allowed to run and play with other dogs or receive affection from people. The only time humans interacted with me was to perform experiments on me. But now I was free. I would never have to return to that life again.

That night, I went home with a very nice family and several of the other dogs. I thought I finally had a family of my own. I later learned that this was just a temporary stop until my forever home could be found.

My forever home came just days later when I went to live with a couple and their pets. I was so excited to have a family of my own, and maybe a little curious, too. They had a cat. And I had never seen a cat before! It turns out I might have been a bit too curious because my forever home wasn't forever.

I went to another home with a woman and her beagle. I was so scared and hid in the corner. I didn't want to go outside or go for walks or play with toys. But she was patient and waited for me to become comfortable. To help me learn safety, she gave me lots of treats! I have been with her and my beagle sister for almost 2 years. She loves me, even when I potty in the house, chew on the furniture or bark at her friends. She lets me sleep in bed with her, under the blanket and right between her legs….my favorite spot! She is my person; my forever home.

Kipper

We first learned of the Beagle Freedom Project through a video clip on CNN more than 5 years ago. That video sparked our motivation to learn more about stopping animal testing and also rescuing a Beagle from BFP. We live in Arizona, and I think our family was one of the first to adopt from BFP outside of California and take a dog to another state. After applying and getting approved, our family flew from Phoenix to Los Angeles to meet Kipper.

Kipper came from Spain and was part of the Spanish 40 Rescue. We met Kipper at Shannon Keith's house and were immediately attached to him. My daughter, who was about 8 years old at the time, was the first person Kipper bonded with. It took him about two weeks in our house before his trust of the adults was evident. Once he settled in, his personality really started to come out and he became more playful by the day.

One of Kipper's favorite things is a stuffed toy donkey that makes donkey noises. He loves to flip it in the air and carry it around. For his birthday, we bought him a dozen of those toys and gave them all to him at one time. He loved it and had fun playing with all of them. If we spread them around the house, he would gather them back to his bed and make sure there weren't any missing.

Kipper also loves going on walks and exploring the neighborhood. It's been really cool seeing him grow and evolve into an adventurer and loving family dog.

Kipper is one of four dogs in our house now. We have adopted a second BFP Rescue named Harry. Having two Beagles from the BFP, both from different origins, we have seen firsthand the potential these dogs have to become loving, trusting pets. It is worth all the effort and time it takes to help rehabilitate them.

They both have certain challenges that surely come from their previous experience and trauma as laboratory subjects, but with enough love and patience, they both have become wonderful family members in our home.

Drummer

Our boy Drummer came from the 9th Beagle Freedom rescue. It was December of 2012, hence, the Christmas themed names for the group. We ended up choosing Drummer out of the bunch because he actually chose us, or at least our son, Jasper, (aged 7 at the time). He stood up on his hind legs and put his front paws on Jasper's stomach, looking up at him with pleading eyes, and there was no more debate over who we'd adopt.

Drummer arrived at our house a few hours later, strung out and sick from a windy trip over the hills via Laurel Canyon. To this day, we haven't had a successful car ride without Drummer getting nauseous. When we do have to take him for a ride, it involves multiple towels, someone holding him with a towel under his chin, and pre-planning the journey via the straightest route. In fact, if we are walking and start to veer in the general direction of a car, Drummer starts to salivate in puddles, like Pavlov's dog,

When Drummer stepped into our house for the first time, we didn't know what to expect - from Drummer, or our 9 year-old shar-pei / pitbull, Muji, or our 11 year old cat, Stoopey. We knew Muji wouldn't be a problem, he's truly the sweetest dog on the planet. The cat, however, was a wild card. Muji was immediately fine with his new little brother. Stoopey was a little more judgmental, but eventually came around. When Drummer first entered the house, he did a fairly brief exploratory, then jumped up, plopped down, and sprawled out on the couch like he'd lived there forever. To this day, he acts like he owns the place.

Having Muji as a big brother was crucial to Drummer's development. It didn't take long to potty train him outside (after a few pee puddles on our TV stand). On our walks, it was instantly clear he'd never been on a leash nor probably even a walk. He didn't seem to get the concept of heading down the sidewalk in one, forward moving direction only, Then I'd see Drummer watch Muji lift his leg on a bush or hunching down on grass, as if he was having some sort of epiphany. Like, "ohhhhh, that's what you do!", and he soon began to copy. He's been good about it ever since, although he still doesn't entirely understand forward momentum, and if allowed, he'll chow down on his own poo. Drummer is a kooky little character, with odd habits that never change.

When he's about to go on a walk, in his excitement, he grabs a toy to chew on. This makes putting the harness on him somewhat challenging, because he refuses to release the toy until we've reached the porch, where he sets it down at the top of the stairs.

Bronco

I first met Cinco at the one-year reunion of the "Spanish 40". I loaded Chief in the truck and made the drive to LA for our reunion party. Forty beagles in a yard free…what could be better? It was the best thing to watch, liberated laboratory beagles everywhere and not one problem.

We were all thinking about our favorite stories to share and making our way into a circle in the center of the yard when I noticed the founder of Beagle Freedom Project, Shannon, speaking with a woman who was in tears.

Not long after, Shannon asked for everyone's attention and proceeded to tell us that Cinco needed a new home. He couldn't get over his incredible fear of the man in the house and was starting to not even want to come home from walks. Of course, I immediately sent a text to my husband explaining the situation. He said only if no one else would take him…We worked out the details and decided Cinco would come to live with us in a few weeks.

Cinco's family brought him out to the ranch where he met our pack and blended right in. He had more physical scars than Chief, a horrible scar on his hind leg and small bald spots on his belly. Bronco, which we soon renamed him, ran from my husband for a short time but got used to him quickly. Even after a year out of the lab Bronco was still afraid of loud noises, especially the fire alarm, and if you tried to pull on him with a leash or his collar he would completely shut down and lay on the ground.

To this day Bronco will run outside if the fire alarm chirps, will throw himself on the ground if you pull on him in any way, and cowers at raised voices. He however, loves squeaky toys and plays like a puppy, is a total cuddler, and loves to go for rides in the car.

Rehabilitated…check!

Bronco

Harry

We have two lab beagles: Kipper and Harry. Kipper was rescued from a lab in Spain. Five months after adopting Kipper from BFP, we traveled to Los Angeles to spend a week volunteering at BFP Headquarters. We had agreed to foster **Harry** and find him a home in Arizona. Harry was part of the San Diego 10 rescue and was in the Spain lab for 7 years. He was more fragile and affected by his time in the lab; and it was apparent from the beginning that he would need a very loving and understanding family to help him recover from the traumas he suffered in the lab.

After only a short time, we were in love with Harry and knew he needed to join our family and spend the rest of his days with us.

Even after being with us for 5 years, Harry is still easily startled by some sounds and motions. He trusts us and knows we love him dearly and will always protect and care for him. He has the sweetest temperament and loves to snuggle. In fact, he's a total bed hog at night. We never knew a little beagle could take up so much room in the bed. He is very friendly with people of all ages likes to meet new people, especially when he's out for a walk. He mostly likes to eat and sleep, though he occasionally has a burst of energy and runs around or plays with toys. He loves to eat popcorn and is very attentive when he smells a bowl of popcorn. Generally speaking, Harry is a homebody. He prefers being at home, relaxing on the couch.

In the morning, he is a slow riser and sometimes stays in bed long after we are up and going. He doesn't come downstairs until his breakfast kibble is poured into his bowl. He will wait at the top of the stairs and listen for the feeding to begin. He only goes outside after his breakfast is finished. Harry is a gentle soul. He definitely has love to give and we can't imagine him being with any other family.

We are blessed to have adopted both Harry and Kipper from the Beagle Freedom Project. We no longer buy products tested on animals. They have recovered from life in the lab and are now happy, healthy beagles. We love them so much and are so blessed to have them in our lives. They both love their lives and are the happiest beagles alive!

Scarlett

Scarlett started her freedom a thin, timid beagle, content to be free but lacking in confidence and with many fears and anxieties. Never uttering a sound, we feared she had been debarked.

We showered her with love, gave her lots of toys, the best of food and a much-deserved place on the bed and couch. Along with twice daily walks in the forest to build her strength and stimulate her senses, this was the least we could do by way of reparations for the sentence she had suffered in the laboratory.

A wonderful transformation then took place. Within days Scarlett's confidence started growing. Within weeks her muscles and stamina built up. A vivacious, cheeky, feisty and strong personality unfolded. At the age of about three, she was experiencing the joys of puppyhood for the first time and became eager to explore the world.

With the help of other dogs, Scarlett learned to play fight and play bite. Then, one day, in a moment of playful mayhem with her cousin Penelope the Pug, she let out a bark of excitement. She had a voice, and what a wonderful voice it was too!

To our surprise, we discovered that Scarlett was not food motivated, it was toys that motivated her. "Is she really a beagle?" some joked. The answer became clear on her "round the block" walk before bedtime when she sighted a fox from the nearby forest: at first, she looked at it quizzically, and then she started baying; "Aroo" … she had found her birthright as a scent hound.

Scarlett still suffers some post-traumatic stress disorder from her days in the laboratory. She doesn't like being covered, is anxious at the start of car journeys and doesn't like loud metallic noises, yet paradoxically isn't perturbed by thunder and lightning. We just shower her with love and try to make every experience a good one. In return Scarlett gives us huge amounts of unconditional love and has changed our lives for the better.

Gilligan

I, like my new sister Cate, used to be known as the tattooed number in my ear. She received her new name Cate after 10 months in the lab. I received my new name, after an estimated 8 years in the lab. You can take your hand away from your mouth, I am a fighter for my cause and my eight years do not define my personality.

Here's how my story starts. A couple of months before I was released and experienced what life really was my family lost a very dear member. Remember, Buddy? That beagle that taught Cate to overcome? He passed away in September. My family was heartbroken. Cate grieved his passing. They found her laying where he would lay and just not being quite herself. Three months later, I was released to my foster family. Which brings me to my introduction. I am Gilligan.

My foster family gave me this name because of my unique personality. I love people. I just want to be loved. I am as they put it, "Everyone's little buddy". Hence, the name Gilligan. Well, a couple of months after adjusting to being out of the lab, my foster family painfully decided I was ready for my forever home. At that exact time, Cate's family decided that they needed to save another life. My life. You see, they figured Buddy helped save Cate, and he lives through her beyond the rainbow bridge. They wanted Cate to save another towards this cause they had become so passionate about. It's funny, though, things didn't go quite as they expected.

I still had my quirks from being in the lab. My paw is bowed and I walk with a little hobble. I had a hard time with transitioning from indoors to outdoors, like Cate. I had a hard time with steps, even falling a few times. The difference- I love to be loved. I love attention. If I see a kid or stranger approach me I am always wagging my tail. Cate is horrified with strangers, but then she sees me approach them, rolling over for rubs and she is curious to see what it is all about.

I am the happiest guy and all I want to do is snuggle on the couch with my humans. I, Gilligan, am an ambassador for lab animals because people can see me and approach me long enough for my humans to tell my story....that even after 8 years in the lab I am so happy to feel love.

Jack

When Jack first arrived, he was very withdrawn, scared, and didn't know what ANYTHING was. While he didn't refuse touch or attention, he didn't seem to think it was friendly, and would not make eye contact. He did pick things up quickly! Learning to drink water from a bowl and eating on his own. While he did break the BFP record for potty training (less than three days) he would not touch the grass for about two weeks. He caught on that going potty outside got you chicken…going inside would not!

I believe Jack suffers from PTSD. He has good days, but more days that show he is still suffering. He has nightmares and still won't make eye contact. He does not like certain things such as flashlights, camera flashes, cords or any kind, and anything that is unfamiliar. We have trained ourselves to keep these things away from Jack. In over 3 years I have only heard Jack bark about six times. He has yet to find his AROOOO. It amazes just how much he still loves people, strangers, and most of all kids.

Jack spent the first year in my bedroom most of the day, his safe room. To get him outside, he needed to be carried to the door and put outside. He couldn't wait to get back inside. This year, his third year outside the lab, is the first year he has enjoyed sitting outside soaking up the sun. This has finally started a turnaround for Jack.

Jack shows love by standing on you…just climbs right up on your chest demanding attention. He does not give kisses but instead gives an "exhale of approval" in your face. He loves to play with ice cubes and will occasionally chew on things like dresser knobs, table legs, and area rugs. He also, now, does a little dance when dinner is served. He will let you know what kind of treat he is in the mood for, hold up one kind, he will turn his head away, second kind, nope…over and over until you present him with the one he has a taste for.

He knows his freedom is special and is using it to free his brothers and sisters

Elvis

When my wife and I received the call to adopt a beagle from Beagle Freedom Project, we knew nothing about the beagle except he was a 3 year-old male rescued from a laboratory in the Memphis area where he had been tested on since he was born. These dogs are basically "born to die". Very few ever get a chance at a real life.

We didn't even have time to book a hotel. We just figured we would find someplace when we got to Memphis. We ended up staying at the Heartbreak Hotel and visited Graceland the next day. Seemed appropriate for Memphis tourists! Then when we went to meet him, fate struck us when we learned his name was, drum roll please, Elvis Presley!

We stayed for hours getting to know his first family. Their story was heart wrenching. They had struggled with infertility and ended up with a "miracle" baby but the baby ended up being highly allergic to dogs so they had no choice but to find a new family for Elvis. We immediately knew Elvis was meant for us. Fate struck again, as we too had struggled for years with infertility.

Rescuing a dog from a laboratory, even though he was three years old, is like getting a puppy but a puppy with PTSD. He was learning basic things at three that he should have learned as a puppy, like how to eat a treat. Let's just say he has found much joy in peanut butter, just like his namesake!

t took over six months but one day, something so basic for a dog was new and strange to him, he learned how to roll around in the grass! We were in tears. We have been able to watch him grow and learn how to be a dog that is loved and appreciated.

Elvis filled a void in our life and there is nothing we wouldn't do for him. As the saying goes, they rescue us just as much as we rescue them. He may not be a human child, but he is our boy, our son we could never have … and we wouldn't have it any other way. He was meant to be ours and we were meant to be his. This love between us is truly everlasting.

Beau

Beau was the most traumatized beagle out of his rescue. All the other beagles released started asking for pets, taking treats, and playing. Beau watched from afar, petrified especially of the men in the room. He was born in the lab; most beagles are purchased from a commercial breeder, and unfortunately this tormented him more. At the breeder, the beagles are at least socialized. Beau, though, was immediately taken from his mom to begin experimentation right away. Even though he was only nine months old when he was liberated, so much damage had already been done.

Once home I held Beau close to me all night long as he trembled, terrified. Although scared he needed to trust someone. From our first day on, I've been the one he runs to whenever he needs comfort. It was six more months before he would let my husband go near him

We figured out Beau loved going on hikes. My husband held Beau's leash on walks so he would associate what he loved with my husband. We were hoping to build some trust. It took over a year for that trust to build only with the help of "walk therapy."

Although Beau remains terrified of people, we are the lucky ones who get to see the true Beau: the goofy pup who loves life and adventure. He is excited every day and views each one as a new exploration. He loves going on hikes for several miles a day. He's very silly and makes us laugh constantly.

Beau and my husband are best buddies now; together they enjoy exploring the woods, jumping in mud puddles, going for a swim in the creek, and chasing geese. Beau sleeps on top of my husband's head at night and you can see Beau following him around throughout the day.

Beau has taught us to live life to the fullest. He's definitely made up for lost time and demands affection (two-handed pets only, please) and adventure all the time. He shows us so much love in return. Because of his resiliency and lust for life, Beau will always be our role model.

Rousseau

Among the 10 beagles rescued from an undisclosed laboratory in the Mid-West, Rousseau was making the trip of 1,500 miles to safety in California with a colossal snow storm right on the heels of the sojourners for much of their journey. He was seven years of age at the time of his rescue, and had the misfortune of coming from a laboratory performing what is called oral gavage. Oral gavage is the protocol where tubes are inserted down the dog's throat and into their stomachs, so that the agent being tested can be administered directly into the digestive system for quick absorption. This is often used in toxicity testing.

As you might expect, many animals going through this process either die directly from the exposure, or are euthanized soon after so that the world at large does not know about this awful process. Occasionally, a lab worker with a conscious will reach out to a rescue organization when the timeline for a testing protocol has been completed. In these rare instances, those lucky, few test subjects will be released. Sadly, beagles are the animals of choice for this sort of testing, as their demeanors are so docile and their natures so trusting! In the winter of 2013, the Beagle Freedom Project was contacted by a lab with a group of older beagles (4 to 10 years of age), who had lived their entire lives in a laboratory cage. None of them had ever seen or smelled the outside world, or had known the touch of a loving hand. But, on February 2013 all of that changed!

Rousseau has the honor of having been named after Dr. Paul Rousseau, who very generously offered to pay for the transportation of these boys to freedom. After all of horrors that these dogs had been though, you might think that the ride to freedom would have been easy by comparison. Mother nature, however, had thrown one more obstacle in their way. As these dogs were being loaded up for transport, the minutes were ticking down to the arrival of a blizzard to hit the Mid-Western states. With the storm bearing ever closer, Rousseau and his lab mates slipped through and finally arrived to freedom at BFP headquarters in Southern California on February 27, 2013. As is true with all such rescues, these boys were able to touch grass for the first time in their lives! Although this is usually a very dramatic change for all laboratory dogs, it was especially so for the Mid-West 10 dogs given that they were all a good deal older and had become very accustomed to lab life.

Indie

We had a beagle when I was about three years old. I've loved beagles ever since.

The first time I heard about Beagle Freedom Project, I immediately wanted to get involved. I started by fostering Barney from the third rescue, and volunteering whenever the opportunity arose. Then, in 2012, BFP rescued a beagle momma and her litter of puppies who had been used for some sort of 'research'. I couldn't get there fast enough! Initially just to help clean up after the puppies and help them get socialized. When they were finally old enough to be fostered, I begged my husband to let me foster one.

Since I would never 'buy' a dog, it might be my only chance to ever have a beagle puppy, even if it was just temporary. Since we already had 5 dogs, I assured him there was no way that we could keep her. To show my gratitude, I even let him name her. He called her Indie. Two weeks later, we signed the adoption papers!

Indie and her sisters are some of the lucky ones. They were so young when they were rescued that they do not struggle with the PTSD that many of these survivor's experience. But as she gets older (she turned five in June 2017), I live with the growing fear of potential side effects from the testing she was subjected to. So many of these sweet survivors have had their lives cut short as a direct result of the unnecessary torture they were forced to endure.

I see in Indie's personality why beagles are a favored breed for research. She LOVES everyone. All I have to do is glance her way and her tail starts to wag and she rolls over for a tummy rub. She insists on meeting every person we pass while out on our walks. To know that this typical beagle characteristic is exploited in such a cruel way is what keeps me fighting for all the animals who suffer in laboratories. There are better options.

Made in the USA
Columbia, SC
19 April 2018